To Sawyer,

Hope y~
Cherris

Cathy Sn

Cheri
A Not So Standard Poodle!

Cathy Smith

Illustrations by Cathy Smith
Design by Lori Duryea

ISBN 978-1-64492-984-1 (hardcover)
ISBN 978-1-64492-985-8 (digital)

Christian Faith Publishing, Inc.
832 Park Avenue
Meadville, PA 16335
www.christianfaithpublishing.com

Printed in the United States of America

This is a tale about my silly poodle, Cheri.
I hope that her mischief and my
drawings make you merry!

Cheri Domino

Minuit

(*Minwee*)

Quite a regal

name for a dog!

But she's really not
very queenly

When she lays on
her back like a frog!

Cheri in French means "sweetheart." And, boy, she sure likes to kiss!

Domino is for the small white spot that appears like a badge on her chest. The rest of her fur is black as midnight (which is *minuit* in French) as you might have already guessed!

Standards are not little poodles (like the ones you might often see).
Cheri is really a big dog, and she stands way up past my knee!

When Cheri was just a little pup, her fur was not all that curly.

But after her first haircut, we called her our new *curly-girly*!

Before Cheri had her first birthday, she didn't behave well at all!
So I decided to take her to obedience school where she might learn to come when we'd call!

Can you imagine how very embarrassed I was after eight week of class

When the dog trainer finally told me that Cheri was *Not* going to pass!

9

For another eight weeks, we both practiced our lessons in sit, heel, and stay.

Our Cher **WON** a second-place ribbon on

Doggie Graduation Day!

2nd Place

She still likes to get into mischief, and you'd never believe all she's done
So just let me tell you a few things this poodle thinks are great fun.

She likes to steal tools from the workmen, who come to work in our house then she brings them things from our hamper, like dirty socks or a blouse!

Once when she'd taken Dad's undershorts,
her legs got caught up in the holes.
So she simply decided to wear
them. For a picture, she
struck quite
the pose!

Then there was the time of Dad's birthday. I had made him his favorite cake. When I had returned from the grocery, Cher had frosting all over her face!

I knew right away what had happened! So I checked how much damage was done.
No wonder she looks so contented, about half the cake was all gone!

Taking trash out of trash cans
is another of Cheri's bad deeds.
But she'll bring
you the trash
if you bribe
her with
one of her
favorite treats!

15

Dad doesn't like this behavior
and gives her a quick
tap on the snout!
Of course, this is
not to her liking,
so she shakes
her head
all about!

Now when she is caught being naughty, her sorrow and shame really shows. She tells us she hopes that we will forgive her when she lays down and covers her nose!

Cher can do tricks for a chewie, which she loves
to sit down and bite!
She'll sit up, shake hands,
and roll over both to
the left

and to the right!

Big poodles are very good hunters,
but Cher's confused about what
she should chase!
She runs after shadows and
reflections. She tries
catching all
over the
place!

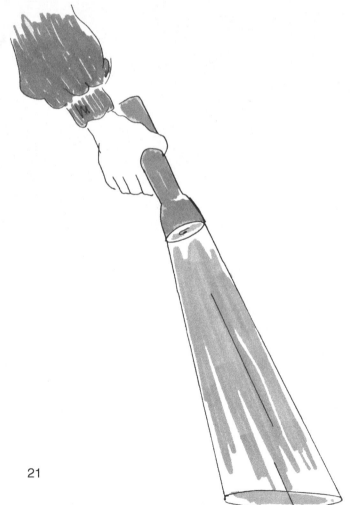

For my son and his friends
(Cheri's a buddy),
She is really just
one of the guys.
With them she
loves to play
football.

23

Her tackles
take them
by surprise!

Sometimes when Cheri is playing,
she pretends she's a big ferocious beast.
She will curl up her lips like she's smiling
and show us her big nasty teeth!

No one is fooled by her snarling
'cause she is so loving and sweet.
If you came to my house for a visit,
she'd jump up and
lick your cheek.

These things
that I have
told you
'bout Cheri,
every word
of my story is
true!

I know if you
ever could meet
her, you'd love
her as much
as I do!

And you know what?
Cher *loves*
you too!

The End.

About the Author

Cathy Smith is a retired registered nurse who has always loved to draw. Now that she is a widow, she decided to take a drawing course at a local community center. It was her very good luck to have an incredible instructor, Lori Duryea, a published illustrator. Since they were discussing cartooning in class, she decided to bring her early attempt at doing a children's book, and with Lori's encouragement and guidance, here she is at seventy-five, having a wonderful new adventure as a published author. SO IT'S NEVER TOO LATE!

CPSIA information can be obtained
at www.ICGtesting.com
Printed in the USA
BVHW020451300519
548967BV00001B/1/P

9 781644 929841